J 821.9

D1136631

Nick Toczek goes swimming and buys things on ebay. He's a poet, magician, storyteller, puppeteer, novelist, comedian, local radio DJ and bald dad. He breeds lizards (bearded dragons, of course!) and likes living in Bradford because he was born there. You can find lots more about him on the Internet. Try putting his name into a good search engine such as Google.

Also by Nick Toczek

Kick It!
Join In or Else
The Dog Ate My Bus Pass

Other books available from Macmillan

Wizard Poems
chosen by Fiona Waters

Guzzling Jelly with Giant Gorbelly
Poems by John Rice

The Monster That Ate the Universe
Poems by Roger Stevens

DRAGONS!

FIRE-BREATHING POEMS
BY NICK TOCZEK

Illustrated by
Sally Townsend

MACMILLAN CHILDREN'S BOOKS

This collection first published 2005 by Macmillan Children's Books
a division of Macmillan Publishers Limited
20 New Wharf Road, London N1 9RR
Basingstoke and Oxford
www.panmacmillan.com

Associated companies throughout the world

ISBN-13: 978-0-330-43744-8
ISBN-10: 0-330-43744-5

Text copyright © Nick Toczek 1996/1998/2005
Illustrations copyright © Sally Townsend 1996/1998

3 5 7 9 8 6 4

A CIP catalogue record for this book is available from
the British Library.

Printed and bound in Great Britain by Mackays of Chatham plc, Kent

CONTENTS

. . . AND SOME RELATIVES OF DRAGONS

THE DRAGON WHO
ATE OUR SCHOOL

The day the dragon came to call,
She ate the gate, the playground wall
And, slate by slate, the roof and all,
The staffroom, gym and entrance hall,
And every classroom, big or small.

So . . .
She's undeniably great.
She's absolutely cool,
The dragon who ate
The dragon who ate
The dragon who ate our school.

Pupils panicked. Teachers ran.
She flew at them with wide wingspan.
She slew a few and then began
To chew through the lollipop man,
Two parked cars and a transit van.

Wow . . . !
She's undeniably great.
She's absolutely cool,
The dragon who ate
The dragon who ate
The dragon who ate our school.

She bit off the head of the head.
She said she was sad he was dead.
He bled and he bled and he bled.
And as she fed, her chin went red
And then she swallowed the cycle shed.

Oh . . .
She's undeniably great.
She's absolutely cool,
The dragon who ate
The dragon who ate
The dragon who ate our school.

It's thanks to her that we've been freed.
We needn't write. We needn't read.
Me and my mates are all agreed,
We're very pleased with her indeed.
So clear the way, let her proceed.

Cos . . .
She's undeniably great.
She's absolutely cool,
The dragon who ate
The dragon who ate
The dragon who ate our school.

There was some stuff she couldn't eat.
A monster forced to face defeat,
She spat it out along the street –
The dinner ladies' veg and meat
And that pink muck they serve for sweet.

But . . .
She's undeniably great.
She's absolutely cool,
The dragon who ate
The dragon who ate
The dragon who ate our school.

DRAGON ON A BUS

Now, you know I'm not a wuss.
I don't like to make a fuss,
But there's just a little matter that I think we
    should discuss . . .
There's a dragon on the bus!
There's a dragon on the bus!
There's a dragon on the bus and it's looking at us!

Let me speak to an inspector
Or the company director
Cos I don't quite recollect a
Sign to say we should expect a
Scaly people-vivisector on this bus.

Now, I never swear and cuss
But it's flipping obvious
That we've got a situation here that could be
    hazardous.
There's a dragon on the bus!
There's a dragon on the bus!
There's a dragon on the bus and it's coming after us!

I think we should call a meeting
Cos its fiery breath is heating
All our clothing and our seating.
I don't like the way it's treating
All the people that it's eating on this bus.

It's chewing us and burning us
And this is what's concerning us.
It could become a problem by the time we reach the
    terminus.
There's a dragon on the bus!
There's a dragon on the bus!
There's a dragon on the bus and it's eating
and it's eating
and it's eating all of us.

DRAGONS ARE BACK

Alas, alack
The dragons are back
And any time now
They're bound to attack.
The sky will turn
From blue to black
With lightning-flash
And thunder-crack.

The dragons are back
The dragons are back
The dragons, the dragons
The dragons are back.

They snap their jaws
Snickerty-snack,
Flash their claws
Flickerty-flack,
Twitch their tails
Thwickerty-thwack,
Clank their scales
Clickerty-clack.

The dragons are back
The dragons are back
The dragons, the dragons
The dragons are back.

The mill goes still.
The wind is slack.
The cows won't milk.
The ducks don't quack.
We try to talk
But just lose track:
Go mumble jumble
Yakkity-yak.

The dragons are back
The dragons are back
The dragons, the dragons
The dragons are back.

We dare not stay.
We quickly pack.
But every road's
A cul-de-sac.
The priest has had
A heart attack.
The king's become
A maniac.

The dragons are back
The dragons are back
The dragons, the dragons
The dragons are back.

THE DRAGON IN THE CELLAR

There's a dragon!
There's a dragon!
There's a dragon in the cellar!
Yeah, we've got a cellar-dweller.
There's a dragon in the cellar.

He's a cleanliness fanatic,
Takes his trousers and his jacket
To the dragon from the attic
Who puts powder by the packet
In a preset automatic
With a rattle and a racket
That's disturbing and dramatic.

There's a dragon!
There's a dragon!
There's a dragon in the cellar!
With a flame that's red 'n' yeller.
There's a dragon in the cellar . . .

. . . and a dragon on the roof
Who's only partly waterproof,
So she's borrowed an umbrella
From the dragon in the cellar.

There's a dragon!
There's a dragon!
There's a dragon in the cellar!
If you smell a panatella
It's a dragon in the cellar.

And the dragon from the study's
Helping out his cellar buddy,
Getting wet and soap-suddy
With the dragon from the loo
There to give a hand too,
While the dragon from the porch
Supervises with a torch.
Though the dragon from the landing,
Through a slight misunderstanding,
Is busy paint-stripping and sanding.

There's a dragon!
There's a dragon!
There's a dragon in the cellar!
Find my dad, and tell the feller
There's a dragon in the cellar . . .

. . . where the dragon from my room
Goes zoom, zoom, zoom
In a cloud of polish and spray-perfume,
Cos he's the dragon whom
They pay to brighten up the gloom
With a mop and a duster and a broom, broom, broom.

There's a dragon!
There's a dragon!
There's a dragon in the cellar!
Gonna get my mum and tell her
There's a dragon in the cellar.

RAGGIN' THE DRAGON

We come right up to the mouth of the cave.
We shout for him as if we're brave.
And he hates the way that we behave.
We make him rant. We make him rave.

We're raggin' the dragon
We're raggin' the dragon
We're givin' the dragon some agony.

Raggin' the dragon is second-to-none.
It's all a game we learn for fun.
We call a name. We turn and run.
We shout: –

'Old slug!
Scabby Lug!
Cave bug!
Ugly thug!

Bag on your head.
Bag on your head.
Face like a dragon,' we said.

Raggin' the dragon is second-to-none.
It's all a game we learn for fun.
We call a name. We turn and run.
We shout: —

'Worm tail!
Beached whale!
Hook nail!
Smelly snail!'

Slaggin' you off.
Slaggin' you off.
'Call yourself a dragon?' we scoff.

Raggin' the dragon is second-to-none.
It's all a game we learn for fun.
We call a name. We turn and run.
We shout: —

'Stink pot!
Body rot!
Hot snot!
Grumpy grot!'

Smack in the snout.
Smack in the snout.
'Raggedy dragon,' is what we shout.

Raggin' the dragon is second-to-none.
It's all a game we learn for fun.
We call a name. We turn and run.
We shout: –

'Green yob!
Slimy slob!
Big blob!
Toothy gob!

Gag on your tongue
Gag on your tongue
Voice like a dragon,' we sung.

Raggin' the dragon is second-to-none.
It's all a game we learn for fun.
We call a name. We turn and run.

We're raggin' the dragon
We're raggin' the dragon
We're givin' the dragon some agony.

THEY'RE OUT THERE

The ghosts of old dragons
Drift over this town,
Their wings grown as thin
As a princess's gown,
Their scaly skin leaf-like
And wintery brown.

The ghosts of old dragons
Are flitting round town.
Their names are lost treasures,
Each glittering noun
Thrown deep in time's ocean
Where memories drown.

The ghosts of old dragons
Keep haunting this town,
Though long gone like gas lamp,
Top hat and half-crown;
Their presence as false
As the face of a clown.

The ghosts of old dragons
Go growling through town,
As upright as tombstones
Engraved with a frown;
With gravel-path voices
Which wind travels down.

TEN GREEN DRAGONS

In the cave dwelt dragons ten.
One fell fighting four horsemen.

In the cave dwelt dragons nine.
One went down the deep, dark mine.

In the cave dwelt dragons eight.
Two forgot to hibernate.

In the cave dwelt dragons six.
One dropped dead from politics.

In the cave dwelt dragons five.
One took a dive in overdrive.

In the cave dwelt dragons four.
One got struck by a meteor.

In the cave dwelt dragons three.
One ran off with a chimpanzee.

In the cave dwelt dragons two.
One went on to the king's menu.

In the cave dwelt dragons one.
Laid ten eggs and then was gone.

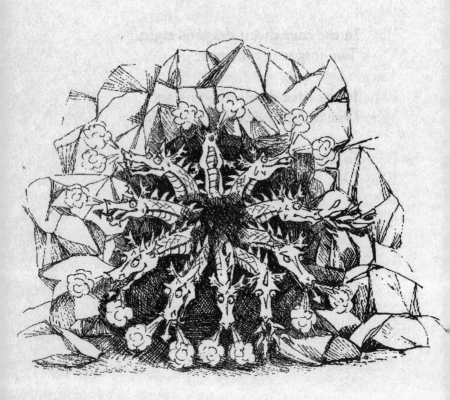

BEING A DRAGON . . .

Being a dragon is as cool as ice.
Being a dragon is nice, nice, nice.
Whatever it costs, it's worth the price
Cos being a dragon is nice.

When you're a dragon, it's fine to fly.
Bag the best wings that money can buy.
Drop 'em in a vat of sky-green dye
Then hang them, bat-like, out to dry.
Shoofly pie, shoofly pie,
When you're a dragon, it's fine to fly.

Being a dragon is as cool as ice.
Being a dragon is nice, nice, nice.
Whatever it costs, it's worth the price
Cos being a dragon is nice.

When you're a dragon, you love your claws.
Use hardware stores when you're stealing yours.
Get stainless ones, cos they're good for wars
Or settling scores, or breaking laws.
Patio doors, patio doors.
When you're a dragon you love your claws.

Being a dragon is as cool as ice.
Being a dragon is nice, nice, nice.
Whatever it costs, it's worth the price
Cos being a dragon is nice.

When you're a dragon, you gargle fire.
Never buy flames, it's better to hire.
Then ignite the tobacco in an old man's briar
And later light his funeral pyre.
Tractor tyre, tractor tyre.
When you're a dragon, you play with fire.

Being a dragon is as cool as ice.
Being a dragon is nice, nice, nice.
Whatever it costs, it's worth the price
Cos being a dragon is nice.

THE WEEK OF THE DRAGON

Monday's dragon was just an egg
Not unlike a chicken's. Were they pulling my leg?

Tuesday's dragon hatched one inch high
With crumpled wings which wouldn't fly
And a roar little more than a squeaky cry.

Wednesday's dragon was the size of a cat
Passers-by paused at the sight of that.
When a woman bent down to give it a pat
It hissed and spat at her and lit her hat.

Thursday's dragon grew bigger than a goat
With a shiny, scaly, bright green coat.
It grew too fast. For an antidote
We saw the vet. But all she wrote was a useless note
Prescribing stuff to cool its throat.

Friday's dragon filled our whole street,
Lamp-posts flattening beneath its feet,
Porches scorched by nostril heat.
It'd eaten all of the butcher's meat
And a child who tried to offer a sweet
And next door's dog as an after-dinner treat.

Saturday's dragon, having learned to fly,
Hovered overhead and blotted out the sky.
Its beating wings, its terrifying cry.
We were all convinced we were about to die,
But luckily for us, my family and I,
None of this happened – let me tell you why:
It WAS a chicken's egg. They'd told me a lie!

So Sunday's dragon wasn't there at all,
Until a strange man, selling eggs, came to call . . .

THE DRAGON'S CURSE

Enter darkness. Leave the light.
Here be nightmare. Here be fright.
Here be dragon, flame and flight.
Here be spit-fire. Here be grief.
So curse the bones of unbelief.
Curse the creeping treasure-thief.
Curse much worse the dragon-slayer.
Curse his purse and curse his payer.
Curse these words. Preserve their sayer.
Earth and water, fire and air.
Prepare to meet a creature rare.
Enter, now, if you dare.
Enter, now . . . the dragon's lair!

DRAGON AT THE SWIMMING POOL

He jumps in with a great big splash.
The waves make several windows smash.
His flame goes out. He coughs grey ash
That lends his lip a thick moustache.

Wings and the water surface crash
Like cymbals giant drummers bash
Or shields when two great armies clash
Or thunder after lightning's flash.

The water's cold. His teeth all gnash.
He shakes his tail, makes it whiplash
Which churns the pool like making mash
And scales break free like scattered cash.

When all four claws begin to thrash
The lifeguard gains a nasty gash,
So swimmers flee, spectators dash.
Panic rules. It's a total hash.

That clumsy beast lacks all panache.
To let him swim was worse than rash.
There should be rules. It's so slapdash.
No dragon ban? That's balderdash!

FINDING A DRAGON'S LAIR

The way to find a dragon's lair
Is down the road that goes nowhere,
Over the bridge of Curse-And-Swear
On the river of Deep Despair.

Take the track to Give-You-A-Scare
Across the marsh of Say-A-Prayer,
Over the peak of Past Repair
And down the cliff of Do Beware.

Through the valley of If-You-Dare
You'll find the town of Don't-Go-There
Where folk don't speak but stand and stare
And nobody will be Lord Mayor.

Beyond lies land that's parched and bare,
A dried-up lake named None-To-Spare,
A rock that's known as Life's Unfair
And hills they call No-Longer-Care.

Dragons

It's hard to breathe the dreadful air
And in the sun's relentless glare
The heat becomes too much to bear.
You'll not be going anywhere.

You're weak and dazed but just aware
Of something moving over there
Approaching to inspect its snare.
And then you smell the dragon's lair.

DRAGONS EVERYWHERE

Mrs Meacher, our gym teacher,
Looks at you like she might eatcha.
Anger alters every feature.
She becomes another creature –
Winged avenger, screamer, screecher.

Burning breath, much more than warm,
She blisters pupils in her form.
If she's a human, I'm a unicorn.

Then there's Gordon, traffic warden,
Ordinary 'n' dull with boredom.
Till he roared 'n' ripped 'n' clawed 'n'
Run amok, all lightning jawed 'n'
Flaming tongued 'n' toothed 'n' clawed 'n'

Frightening as a thunderstorm.
But underneath his uniform
If there's a human, I'm a unicorn.

Mrs Ritter, babysitter,
TV watcher, silent knitter.
I know why her clothes don't fit her.
She's another fire-spitter,
Beastly, battle-scarred and bitter.

Her bat-like wings have both been shorn,
But I know that she's dragon spawn.
If she's a human, I'm a unicorn.

Mouseman Mervyn, dressed in rat skin,
Brings his traps in, catches vermin.
Scratches his reptilian chin
With fingernails grown long and thin.
His bloodshot eyes, his evil grin.

A twisted figure, worn and torn,
Who can't recall where he was born.
If he's a human, I'm a unicorn.

Miss McPeake, our glum shopkeeper,
Avaricious treasure-heaper,
Piles 'em high and sells them cheaper.
People-server and floor-sweeper,
Deep down, though, she'd be Grim Reaper.

Customers all sense her scorn.
One day they'll meet her with claws drawn.
If she's a human, I'm a unicorn.

The family that lives next door
Seem quite all right, but nightly roar
And smoke stains ruin their decor.
And each of them's a carnivore –
I've seen them eating meat that's raw.

A mountain cave on the Matterhorn
Is where each first saw the light of dawn.
If they're all human, I'm a unicorn.

And as for me, I'm feeling strange,
All aches and pains and bad migraines.
Soon parts of me will start to change,
My limbs and body rearrange,
And I'll become quite dangerous,

Grow rows of teeth like rose-bush thorns
And skin as tough as rhino horn,
And be a dragon, not a unicorn.

BLUBBERBELLY WOBBLEWALK STUMBLEBUM SMITH

When I was young, I made friends with
Blubberbelly Wobblewalk Stumblebum Smith,
A proper live dragon, not just a myth.

Lonely and large as a monolith,
Blubberbelly Wobblewalk Stumblebum Smith
Had no parents, kin or kith.

One day I was cruel. He left forthwith,
Blubberbelly Wobblewalk Stumblebum Smith,
For a secret place he called his frith.

I often wish I'd made up with
Blubberbelly Wobblewalk Stumblebum Smith,
Who never returned after our daft tiff.

Was he real, or merely a myth?
Blubberbelly Wobblewalk Stumblebum Smith,
The dragon I used to be friends with.

THE CHILD WHO PRETENDED TO BE A DRAGON

My mum and dad got angry
And they told me not to lie,
When I said that I'd grown wings
And was learning how to fly.

They said I should be sensible
And stop making a fuss,
After I'd announced that I was green
And longer than a bus.

And they turned around and told me
I was not to tell tall tales,
When they heard I'd been claiming
That my skin was growing scales.

Then both of them got cross with me
And each called me a liar,
Just because I mentioned
I'd been breathing smoke and fire.

But they finally got flaming mad,
They really hit the roof,
When I rushed at them with sharpened claws
And all my teeth, as proof.

My mum let out a piercing scream.
My dad began to rave.
So I ate them both. They tasted nice.
Then I flew off to live in a cave.

DRAGON

Dragon has spikes all down her back,
Has claws in her paws that she draws to attack.
She's scaly, savage and sickly green,
Merciless, mindless, cruel and mean.

Dragon is heartless, has no soul.
Her red eyes glow like burning coal.
A body that's built with bulletproof scales.
She can pound you to pulp with a swish of her tail.

Dragon has a furnace fitted in each lung,
A flickering, forked and fireproof tongue,
Crocodile jaws from which she pours
Great searing flames, with frightful roars.

Dragon's cave is a reeking trench
With a dank, sulphurous, smoky stench
Made fouler by the crevices and cracks
Where rotting limbs are stored for snacks.

Dragon loves her cavernous lair,
Keeps her heaps of treasures there,
Hardly sleeps for fear of thieves,
Needs to be ravenous before she leaves.

When dragon spreads her dreadful wings
Death will be what her hunger brings.
Breathlessly she pursues warm flesh.
She wants it human, young and fresh.

Dragon spies people far beneath.
She flies down, claws first, followed by teeth.
She grips and grinds. She chomps and chews.
She spits out belt buckles, buttons and shoes.

Dragon finally finishes feeding
Splatter red from all their bleeding,
Flies home slowly with a bloated gut,
Reaches the entrance to her darkness . . . but . . .

Dragon senses men and horses,
Sniffs the air . . . sniffs then pauses . . .
A stink, she thinks, not normally there . . .
A man, somewhere inside her lair!

When a dragon stares into her breath,
Her life up to the point of death
Appears before her in the smoke –
The future pulling back its cloak.

Dragon breathes . . . The picture clears
But it lacks its usual months and years.
Instead she sees reflected back
Mere moments, then a sea of black.

Dragon-slayer draws his bow,
Aims, and lets his arrow go.
It flies to where the scaly coat
Is weakest, at the creature's throat.

Dragon feels the fatal flood,
The sea of black, the flow of blood,
And, far below, the undertow
Of pain, from bolt and piercing blow.

Dragon falls and twists about.
Her fire chokes and flickers out.
She coughs a cloud of smoke. She sighs,
Then lies quite still, with staring eyes.

The slayer slices off her head
To make quite certain that she's dead.
These killings bring him little pleasure.
He never dares to touch their treasure.

He doesn't like the job as such.
It doesn't earn him very much.
And with each dragon, goes a curse,
So death by death, his life grows worse.

Why does he do it? you may ask.
Well, someone has to do the task.
He breaks her eggs. He blocks her cave.
He buries her body in a shallow grave,
Shoves the head in a blood-stained sack
And leads his horse back down the track.

SCALY SKIN

I have a toothsome evil grin
And blood around my lips and chin
That is of human origin.
It trickles down my scaly skin.

I've eyes as sharp as any pin.
They're hard and red and dark as sin.
I'm roguish as a Rasputin:
A devil in a scaly skin.

My roar's a deep explosive din
That mixes nitroglycerine
With flaming tongues of paraffin
So hot they scorch my scaly skin.

My cries that rise so high and thin –
Like madness on a violin
Or bagpipes with no discipline –
Send shivers down my scaly skin.

But I've a toothsome evil grin
And blood around my lips and chin
That is of human origin.
It trickles down my scaly skin.

MAKING MY
DRAGON GUFFAW

It's easy to make
My dragon laugh.
Just tell her a joke
That's terribly naff,
Or take her to work
And say to the staff:
'I'd like you to meet
My green giraffe.'
And then my dragon'll
Loudly laugh

And laugh and laugh
And laugh and laugh.

It's easy to make
My dragon guffaw.
Just tell her: 'I'm told
By people that you're
A crocodile crossed
With a dinosaur.'
My dragon'll give
A great big guffaw,
A doubly deafening
Giggly roar

And roar and roar
And roar and roar

Till throat and jaw
Are stiff and sore
And scales galore, galore, galore
Are scattered around her on the floor . . .

Guffaw, guffaw,
Guffaw, guffaw . . .

MAYBE YOU'RE A DRAGON

If your voice is grumpy
If your claws are clumpy
If your back is bumpy
Maybe you're a dragon.

If your cheeks are chumpy
If your tail is thumpy
If your head is humpy
Maybe you're a dragon.

If your body's dumpy
If your waddle's rumpy
If your breath is trumpy
Maybe you're a dragon.

If your legs are stumpy
If your shape is frumpy
If your tummy's plumpy
Maybe you're a dragon.

If your skin is mumpy
If your jaws are jumpy
If your face is lumpy
Maybe you're a dragon.

ROARING LIKE DRAGONS

On the count of four, I want you all to roar.
One . . . two . . . three . . . four . . .

No! Not the squawk of a fowl,
Or the hoot of an owl,
Or the half-choked note of a bleating goat,
Or the moody moo that a cow'll do.
That was very, very poor.
I fare better when I snore.
What I want is a proper roar.
One . . . two . . . three . . . four . . .

No, no, no! Not a toothsome scowl,
Or a long, loud vowel,
Or the screech of creatures
When a beast is on the prowl.
Call that your best? I'm far from sure.
It didn't thrill me to the core.
Now gimme a roar I can't ignore.
One . . . two . . . three . . . four . . .

Pathetic! Did I ask for a yell or a yelp or a yowl?
Did I call for a caterwaul, holler or howl,
Or a burp or a belch
From a belly or a bowel?
Now rattle the windows and the door.

Shake the ceiling and the floor,
Show your jaw what your lungs are for.
One . . . two . . . three . . . four . . .

Hmm. That felt fierce and forcefully foul.
I'd call that a fabulously fearsome growl.
But did it rip your lips up?
No! Did it jellify your jowl?
No! Well, sorry to be a bit of a bore.
But I think you can guess what I've got in store . . .
That I'm going to ask you for even more.
So be louder than the crowd when the home team
  score.
Make a shock wave worse than the Third World
  War.
Do astounding sounds, like dragons galore.
Roar and roar as never before.
Roar and roar till your throats are sore.
One . . . two . . . three . . . four . . .

Encore!

Encore!!

Encore!!!

THE AMERICAN DRAGON

Elephantine, with a burger belly,
He sits in New York, watching telly –
A graceless beast in a room that's smelly.

This figure far bigger than a Botticelli
Is fed fatty food from his local deli –
Fries and pizzas and tagliatelli.

His weak wings flap like a pair of umbrelli,
For a flightless wobble by a bright green jelly
With more spare tyres than anyone requires . . .
. . . even the suppliers of Pirelli!

He's jealous of the elegance of Gene Kelly
And longs to be lithe like Liza Minnelli
Or to flaunt a physique like football's Pele.

But elephantine, with a burger belly,
He sits in New York, watching telly –
This graceless beast in a room that's smelly.

SONG OF THE DRAGON-SLAYER

Oh, the only good dragon
The only good dragon
The only good dragon's a dead 'un.

From mystic, pre-Christian, weaving and threading,
Great Worm that is winter-sky grey, grim and
   leaden,
Through winged English Green and rapacious
   Welsh Red 'un
To deceptively decorous Orient-bred 'un.

The only good dragon
The only good dragon
The only good dragon's a dead 'un.

I take drastic action to stop 'em from spreading,
The ground all around is left darkened and bled-on
My blade hacks their necks till each beast has no
   head on,
So saving the souls they would surely have fed on.

The only good dragon
The only good dragon
The only good dragon's a dead 'un.

FINDING A DRAGON THAT'LL FINISH OUR FOOD

We're children. We're choosy.
We're fussy. We're picky.
Don't want food that's oozy
Or slimy or sticky.
Leave heaps and whole slices
From each of those courses
You serve up in spices
Or herbs or thick sauces.
Whatever you make us,
Just count yourself lucky
If we don't pull faces
Or moan that it's yucky.

Yet you say that it's rude of us, leaving our food.
But who'll nosh our noodles or feed on our peas?
We need a fine dragon who'll dine on all these:
Our spam, spuds and spinach, our strong stinky
    cheese,
Lentils and lettuces, pale tripe and mustard,
Large lumpy dumplings and great globs of custard.

You'd best find a beast that you know licks its lips
At kippers and leeks and asparagus tips,
Parsnips and turnips and marrows and swedes,
Haggises, cabbages, cress and such weeds.
With luck, it'll suit the great big-bellied brute
To pig out on pork pies and purple beetroot.
And bring us a beastie to sit up and beg
For the runniest bits of a breakfast boiled egg.

We're children. We're choosy.
We're fussy. We're picky.
Don't want food that's oozy
Or slimy or sticky.

So drag out a dragon that's certain to rid me
Of slithery liver and leathery kidney,
Who sometimes devours entire cauliflowers,
A dragon quite barmy for brawn or salami,
Mad about marrows, mincemeat, minestrone,
Prunes, prawns and porridge and cold macaroni.
We need, now, a creature who'd be cock-a-hoop
For oysters and olives and old oxtail soup,
A beast keen on onions and dark aubergines,
Broccoli, rhubarb and heaps of broad beans,
Cockles and mussels and salady greens,
Horseradish sauce and whole tins of sardines.

Whatever you make us,
Just count yourself lucky,
If we don't pull faces
Or moan that it's yucky.

Please help us to find a fine beast of this kind
Who'll finish off platefuls of thick bacon rind,
A great gherkin-gobbler, a greedy and good 'un,
Who'll eat up our meatballs and see off black
puddin',
A huge hot-breath creature who, quite without
worries,
Could casually swallow the strongest of curries.
Yes, we've a fine feast for a full-bellied beast
Who'll merrily munch on a big bunch of celery.
Why, I bet a dragon's great fireproof snout
Could even consume an entire Brussels sprout.

We're children. We're choosy.
We're fussy. We're picky.
Don't want food that's oozy
Or slimy or sticky.

But give us a dragon that's willing to eat
Our vilest of veges, our fattiest meat,
Our foulest of fruits, our unsavoury sweet,
And mealtimes would magically turn out a treat.

A POEM TO WHISPER

Shhh!

All the dragons are fast asleep,
Each curled up on a golden heap
Of treasure that these creatures keep.

Shhh!

All the dragons are fast asleep.
Their cave is dark. Their cave is deep –
A chimney stack we've come to sweep.

Shhh!

All the dragons are fast asleep.
We crowd outside like silent sheep
And warily, by torchlight, peep.

Shhh!

All the dragons are fast asleep.
With weapons in our hands we creep
Down corridors cut cold and steep.

Shhh!

All the dragons are fast asleep.
We reach their lair and start to reap,
And each one dies without a peep.

Shhh!

All the dragons are fast asleep
And rivulets of red blood seep
Through riches, proving life is cheap.

Shhh!

All the dragons are fast asleep
And, though my friends all whoop and leap,
For some strange reason I could weep.

Shhh!

ACTING AS IF
WE'RE DRAGONS

Let's imagine that we're dragons. See who's best.
Pretend you're fast asleep inside your nest . . .
Then stretch as you emerge from reptile rest . . .
Yawn . . . and growl from deep inside your
  chest . . .
Press your stomach . . . Dream of something to
  digest . . .

Shake yourself . . . and breathe out thick, black
  smoke . . .
Cough a bit . . . because it makes you choke.
Then rub your eyes . . . and move like you just
  woke . . .

Slowly stare out from your mountain lair . . .
Snarl . . . and try to make your nostrils flare . . .
Now suck . . . to fill your fiery lungs with air . . .

Let's see you exercise your lethal claws . . .
Expose those rows of teeth between your jaws . . .
Then scratch your ancient scars from dragon
  wars . . .

Stand up slowly . . . huge and hard as nails.
Flex those muscles underneath your scales . . .
Now set your sights on distant hills and vales . . .

And flap your arms as if they're heavy wings . . .
Listen to the way the high wind sings . . .
As you fly towards the lands of kings.

Lick your lips . . . and keep your cruel eyes peeled . . .
Though you need to feed, your wounds have
   hardly healed
From your fight with a knight with sword and shield.

You're dizzy and weak before you arrive.
This time, you wonder if you will survive.
It's dangerous to hunt in the human hive.

But hunger hurts, it stabs your guts like five
   hundred knives.
See that food below you . . . ? Go into a dive . . .
Rip apart everything down there alive.

THE MYTH OF CREATION

A dragon flew out of the sun
And from its flames whole worlds were spun
And from its names were words begun
With all we've thought and said and done
And wars were fought and lost and won
And tales were taught and lies were spun
That a dragon flew out of the sun.

WHAT HAVE WE GOT
IN THE HOUSE?

I think I know what we've got in the house.
When it moves, it makes more mess than a mouse.
So, what do you think we've got in the house?

We found eggshell down
By the washing machine
And four claw-prints
In the margarine.

I think I know what we've got in the house.
When it moves, it makes more mess than a mouse,
Or a rat, or a roach, or a louse.
So, what do you think we've got in the house?

The sides of the bath
Are greenish-tinged
And the spare toothbrush
Has had its bristles singed.

I think I know what we've got in the house.
When it moves, it makes more mess than a mouse.
Or a rat, or a roach, or a louse,
Or a gerbil, or an oyster, or a grouse.
So, what do you think we've got in the house?

We've never had a fire
But I often cough.
Then the smoke alarm
In the hall goes off.

I think I know what we've got in the house.
When it moves, it makes more mess than a mouse.
Or a rat, or a roach, or a louse,
Or a gerbil, or an oyster, or a grouse,
Or a duck-billed platypus together with its spouse.
So, what do you think we've got in the house?

There are long scratch marks
Just like from claws
Around the handles
Of all the doors.

I think I know what we've got in the house.
Don't you?

THE SOUND OF SLEEPING DRAGONS

Asleep on deep dark dungeon floors,
Our dragons dream, like dinosaurs,
Their wordless reveries of roars . . .

A punctuation of bold snores
That grumbles out of gaping jaws
And tumbles down cold corridors.

The sound of sleeping,
Sound of sleeping,
Sound of sleeping dragons.

It rumbles round their treasure stores.
It crumbles roofs. It rattles doors.
It leaks outside like loud applause.

It echoes over lakes and moors.
It crests the peaks where eagle soars
To fade beyond the farthest shores.

The sound of sleeping,
Sound of sleeping,
Sound of sleeping dragons.

LIFE AND DEATH

They felt few emotions.
Their blood was corrosive.
Their dreams were deep oceans.
Their breath was explosive.

Their land lay uncharted.
Their caves were like sewers.
Their sleep was hard-hearted.
Their claws were like skewers.

Their hunger was boundless
Their lives, melodrama.
Their flight was quite soundless.
Their scales were their armour.

Their tails were like rivers.
Their flames like bright fountains.
Their cries caused cold shivers.
Their wealth was worth mountains.

Their instinct was grasping.
Their airspace was birdless.
Their voices were rasping.
Their language was wordless.

Their eyes were like lasers.
Their minds were infernal.
Their teeth were like razors.
Their wisdom eternal.

Their fighting ferocious.
Their battleground blazing.
Their deaths were atrocious,
Though they were amazing.

MODERN DRAGONS

Modern dragons act all flash,
Swish around with wads of cash,
Splash out rashly, dish the dosh,
Push for posh and pricey nosh.

They've more money than they've senses,
Have expensive residence,
High-class caves to suit the choosy –
Bidet, sauna and jacuzzi.
Wall-to-wall, these works of art
Are sumptuous, deluxe and smart.

Modern dragons of both sexes
Need fine jewellery, nice Rolexes,
Diamonds on their necks and wrists,
Gold rings clustered round their fists,
Pearl-encrusted treasure chests
Thrust in niches in their nests.

Modern dragons, draped in jewels,
Laze by heated swimming pools,
Sip Barcardis and Martinis,
Lounge around in Lamborghinis.
There's not much they can't afford
And all their claws are manicured.

Modern dragons own racehorses,
Drive to parties in green Porsches
Or Ferraris or Rolls-Royces,
Talk in crisp and cultured voices,
Carve out consonant and vowel.
Modern dragons never growl.

With bodylines all redefined
Our dragons now are quite refined.
They've had their awkward wings removed.
They call it 'surgically improved'.
They've also been unspiked, untailed,
Their skins made paler and descaled,
Body-fat redistributed,
Teeth filed flat, false hair recruited.

Snakeskin booted, silken suited,
They socialize, their fire muted.

Modern dragons cruise and jet.
They never work. They never sweat.
Their world is one devoid of debt
Where anything they want, they get –
A world so small, there is no threat.
They never need to get upset.
The only things that make them fret
Are status, style and etiquette.

THE BIRTH OF A DRAGON

Into the belly of the nest
She'd built in the bleak northwest
The mother dragon pressed
An egg as big as a whisky keg.

And leaves grew dark on oak and yew,
While her offspring fed on yolk, and grew.
Then a crack in the shell and, poking through
Came a claw, a few more, then a leg.

And the whole egg broke in two
And from the shell came half the smell of Hell

And with it a beast without place or time,
Like a word which will not write or rhyme.
So there it lay, encased in slime,
For a while, then raised a head that was vile.

No natural nightmare could compile
This child, with eyes as wide and wild
As the seas which swirl around all these isles,
And a cry which reaches miles and miles.

And lightning, flashing over beaches,
Comes from flaming, flickering tongues;
While thunder, galloping from lungs,
Terrorizes creatures.

THE MISUNDERSTOOD DRAGON

If we meet with a dragon while out walking in this
    wood,
I can't help wondering whether we should
Automatically assume that he's up to no good.

Admittedly, he'd drag us off and doubtless would
Make a meal of us both as quickly as he could,
Crunching on our bones and licking up the blood
For supper, with gravy and mounds of mashed spud
And cabbage and carrots and Yorkshire pud.

And we'd land in a lump in his stomach with a
    thud
And slip with a squelch into pools of tummy crud,
Like splashing in your wellies in a puddle of mud.
But he'd belch and say, 'Sorry!' as we sank in that
    flood.
He's not cruel – just hungry, and a bit
    misunderstood.

HOW THE DRAGON BECAME HEROIC

That vicious rapscallion
Grew colder and harder,

Dragged knight from his stallion
With relish and ardour,

Slew German, Italian
And Dane for his larder,

Drove back a battalion
From here to Granada,

Sank each Spanish galleon
That formed the Armada,

To earn a medallion
As our nation's guarder.

WHAT THE DRAGON THOUGHT

I'm finer than a dinosaur
For few of them have wings to soar
And none have my incendiary roar
And I can dine on so much more.
I'm one voracious carnivore . . .
But fate awaits with larger jaw.

I'm finer than a dinosaur.
Their world seems new, so they explore,
But I have seen it all before.
I'm old and wise. They're immature.
I cogitate. They just guffaw
As though their heads were full of straw.

I'm finer than a dinosaur.
The future's something they ignore.
To me, though, it's an open door
Where years come like a corridor,
Our footsteps fading from its floor,
Just scrubbed away . . . a servant's chore.

I'm finer than a dinosaur.
The light is dim. My eyes are sore
But I can see what lies in store.
We'll all die out. I know the score.
Our genes possess a fatal flaw
For which our bodies know no cure.

I'm finer than a dinosaur.
But what is all my wisdom for?
It only leaves me insecure
And melancholic to the core,
The way the truth can slowly gnaw
Till every thought feels red and raw.

A SEASON FOR DRAGONS

Between childhood and fairy tales
Stretch wonderment and winding trails,
Through summer days and wooded dales
Where leaves grow green as dragon scales.

But, as we age, the picture pales,
Of maidens, knights and Holy Grails.
The 'I've-no-time-for-that' prevails
To dull the colours and details.

Great shadows fall on hills and vales,
As clouds more corpulent than whales
Roll overhead on wings like sails
That beat the air like threshing flails.

And branches thrash like serpents' tails,
And summer somersaults and fails,
While winds are whipped to autumn gales
That howl the way a creature wails.

Hollow as caves from which it hails,
Comes burning breath this beast exhales.
The tongue of flame that this entails
Leaves leaves as brown as rusted nails.

HOW DRAGONS
HIDE FROM US

Dragons Portuguese and Spanish,
Like the Cheshire Cat, can vanish.
Russian dragons, though they're large,
Are very skilled at camouflage.
And Chinese dragons, to escape,
Become old folk by changing shape.

Dragons northern European,
Caribbean and Andean,
Hebridean and Fijian,
Galilean and Korean
Can shrink until they're minuscule
Then hide beneath a small toadstool.

Those from Corfu and Katmandu,
Mogadishu, Timbuktu,
Honolulu, Timaru,
And Machu Picchu in Peru,
Plus a few from Gazankulu
And one who's called Bartholemew
Can turn transparent, quite see-through.

While English dragons, being green,
Can hide in envy, quite unseen.
But their Welsh cousins, painted red,
Can't hide at all. So they're all dead.
Yet dragons from the USA
Just scream at us and run away.

THE DEATH OF A SCOTTISH DRAGON

A young

Dragon named Keith,
With hundreds of teeth
Above and beneath

His tongue,

Lived north of Leith
Till killed on the heath
Near cold Cowdenbeath.

They flung

Earth onto Keith
Took a sword from its sheath
And on it a wreath

Was hung.

PUB TALK

In the bar of the George and Dragon
They'll serve you a foaming flagon
Of English ale
And tell you a tale
Of battling beasts and of bragging.

Swaggering knights, given a scragging,
In agony staggering, bloodied and flagging,
Fall dead or dying,
Cruel fate denying
Them victory over the dragon.

Now, drinking is good at ungagging,
And legend set local tongues wagging . . .
That old dragon's den,
Seen by pit-rescue men,
Had many a full moneybag in.

For hundreds of years it's had swag in,
Since Georgie, a young scallywag in
A suit of cheap tin
Did the dreadful beast in,
With no sword, just a bread-knife zigzagging.

In the bar of the George and Dragon
They'll serve you a foaming flagon
Of English ale
And tell you a tale
Of battling beasts and of bragging.

THE BEASTLY DRAGON

The dragon, the dragon's a beastly beast,
Its face all crumpled up and creased.
It should be jailed and not released,
Instead it's out there, unpoliced.

The dragon, the dragon's a beastly beast,
A fire-breathing, winged artiste
That's dangerous, to say the least.
It thinks of people as a feast.

The dragon, the dragon's a beastly beast
That has no faith in church or priest,
And though their numbers have decreased,
They're still out west and in the east.

The dragon, the dragon's a beastly beast
That feeds on food that's not deceased,
Till caked in blood and thoroughly greased,
Its temper worse, its size increased.

The dragon, the dragon's a beastly beast.
From life that's found in lumps of yeast,
To rhino, whale or wildebeest,
The dragon, the dragon's the beast of beasts.

EVIDENCE

Dragon in computer games.
Places bearing dragon names.
Dragon used as skin tattoo.
Ship to carry Viking crew.
Sleeping now, but when it wakes,
Starts up storms and makes earthquakes.

Dragon drawn on early maps.
Gardens where the dragon snaps.
Ponds patrolled by dragonflies.
Dragon donning human guise.
Serpent circling the globe.
Dragon on a Chinese robe.

Dragon flown as paper kite.
Effigy in tribal rite.
Dragon as a kids' cartoon.
Origin of world 'dragoon'.
Dragon that the hero slew.
Biggest thing that ever flew.

Dragon landing on your roof.
You still saying: 'Bring me proof!'

GOODNIGHT, GOOD KNIGHT

When sunset came
To Hungry Wood,
Dragon so bad
Met knight so good.
A fight began
Where these two stood.

When daybreak came
To Hungry Wood,
Dragon chewed on
Berries for pud
And said, 'Yum-yum,
Last knight was good!'

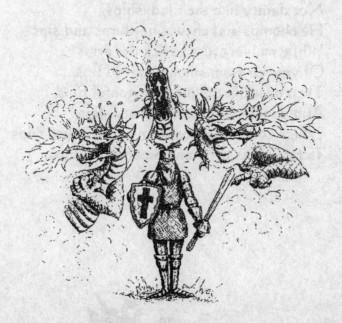

DRAGON EATING FISH-N-CHIPS

Watch dragon scoffing fish-n-chips.
He slashes with his claws and rips
The paper wrapping off in strips,
Reveals his meal and promptly dips
Right in with eager talon-tips,
Locates his target, grabs and grips
Scissor-like with snickerty-snips,
And lobs each load between his lips,
Like building workers loading skips.

Hear dragon gobble fish-n-chips.
Not dainty like their ladyships,
He chomps and chews, he slurps and sips
While pausing just to lick the drips
Of vinegar from smoke-stained lips.
Then past his tongue each gobful flips
And down his throat it loudly slips
Where countless meals have made such trips
To fatten his belly and broaden his hips.

When dragon wolfs down fish-n-chips,
Such is his greed, he often strips
Potato farms and fishing ships.
He's like some vast apocalypse
That steals our food, that nicks, that whips,
That no disaster can eclipse.
'Today, I ate your fish-n-chips.
Tomorrow, I shall dine . . .' he quips,
'On people-meat!' and smacks his lips.

TROGLODYTIC
OWNER-OCCUPIER

Old flier with a bellyful of fire
That's hotter than a deep-fat-fryer,
Your tongue is tougher than a tyre,
Thicker and harder and drier.
You've the appetite of a vampire.

Old flier with a bellyful of fire,
You're driven by desire to acquire.
You trickster, rogue and liar.
You've eyes like snakes', but slyer.
They're sharp as thorns on briar.

Old flier with a bellyful of fire,
Mister mayhem multiplier.
Your cry's a terrifier,
The sound of a suffering choir
Entangled in barbed wire.

Old flier with a bellyful of fire,
Soaring higher than church and spire.
You're lord and magnifier,
His dragonship, esquire,
Arrogant, for all to admire.

SPEAKING DRAGONESE

And do you do just as you please?
And are you keen on killing sprees?
And do you speak in Dragonese?

Do you, as everyone agrees,
Enjoy these joyless jamborees,
Pursuing everyone who flees,
A heartless sword of Damocles
Descending on these refugees?
And do you speak in Dragonese?

And of the people whom you seize,
Do you chew through each of these
As though they were just chunks of cheese?
And are your legs like trunks of trees,
Your hide as hard as manganese?
And do you speak in Dragonese?

Are you immune to most disease,
An unkind kind of Hercules,
A piece of slime, a slice of sleaze,
Whose mind despises all it sees
Through eyes as cold as dungeon keys?
And do you speak in Dragonese?

Does weather warm a few degrees
Whenever you so much as sneeze?
And is your breath the devil's breeze,
A howling, haunted, heated wheeze,
A wind to blow till Hell shall freeze?
And do you dream in Dragonese?

THE WORST SMELL IN THE WORLD . . . EVER!

The stench of a dragon
Has no parallel.
That stink has a tag on
That reads: 'Made in Hell!'

Your feet begin dragging.
You're feeling unwell.
You're coughing and gagging.
You choke and you yell.

When you're near a dragon
Your nostrils rebel.
Your nose is in agony
Due to the smell.

Your senses start sagging.
Your brain'll soon swell.
Its processes flagging,
Destroyed, cell by cell.

The smell of a dragon
Is one I know well.
If you think I'm bragging
Just sniff. Can you tell?

You stagger, zigzagging,
My breath a bombshell,
Because I'm a dragon.
Now bid life farewell!

WHY WELSH DRAGONS
STOPPED BEING GREEN

I know why all dragons in Wales
Are red from their heads to their tails.
They once lived in trees.
Up there, by degrees,
They ripened, then fell, with red scales.

WHAT REG SAYS

There are still some dragons,
Or so Reg alleges.
Some nest inaccessibly
On mountain ledges,
Or in polar regions
Not accessed by sledges,
Or hidden in marshland
By tall reeds and sedges.

And sometimes you find them,
Or so Reg alleges,
In caves under oceans
At depths no one dredges,
Or in crumbling castles
Behind walls and hedges
With 'KEEP OUT!' and 'PRIVATE!' signs
All round the edges.

And some live down our way,
Or so Reg alleges,
Their neighbours all made to
Sign secrecy pledges.
These creatures eat pizzas,
Potato fried wedges,
And chicken and burgers
And stuff cooked for veggies.

And sometimes small people . . .
Or so Reg alleges.

THE STRENGTH OF DRAGONS

All them dragons, 'ard as nails,
Bend steel girders wi' their tails,
Green in England, red in Wales,
'omes in caves and dungeon jails
That reek of smoke and old entrails,
'oarding gold and guarding grails,
Wingspan wide as galleon sails.

All them dragons, tough as bricks,
'atched from eggs, like nestling chicks,
Eyes as cold as old oil slicks.
Vandalizing lunatics,
They knock 'ole villages for six,
'eadbutt castle walls for kicks
And smash 'em up like matchsticks.

All them dragons, built like boots,
Bullet-proof in scaly suits,
Are cruel and calculating brutes.
Night-time flights down secret routes
To meet up cos they're in cahoots.
Vile and vicious in disputes
They share nefarious pursuits.

All them dragons, rough as rocks,
Anarchic and unorthodox,
'ave body parts like concrete blocks.
Each 'as a gob o' teeth that locks
Like thief-proof vault or strongbox.
These beasts gang up in flaming flocks
And armoured knights are laughing stocks.

THE DISAPPEARANCE OF CHINESE DRAGONS

Three thousand miles from the Philippine Isles
To the heights of Turkistan,
And all the way from Mandalay
To the coast of far Japan

You'll find depicted and displayed
Dragons of every shape and shade
Embroidered, painted, carved in jade,
In ivory, pearl or wood-inlaid.
Their past was treasure. Their future's trade.
They're only worth the price that's paid.

From copper mines and camel lines
On dry Mongolia's barren plains
To Buddhist prayer and Yeti lair
On high Tibetan mountain chains

The dragon that they now parade's
A paper one which people made.
The actual creature's long decayed,
Its spirit cheapened and betrayed
With paste and paint that time will fade;
Its world of wonderment mislaid.

Three thousand miles from the Philippine Isles
To the heights of Turkistan,
And all the way from Mandalay
To the coast of far Japan

No egg, no bone, no trace remains.
An empty throne where silence reigns.
A twilight zone. All loss, no gains.
The bird has flown. The old moon wanes.
No crop is grown: no fruit, no grains.
Its ghost is blown through those terrains.

MOODY DRAGON

Look back there. That's where he's laggin'
Way behind us, moanin', naggin'.
Oh, just listen to that dragon
Sayin', 'Slow down, please. I'm flaggin'!

Seekin' pity. Blag-blag-blaggin'.
Sympathy he thinks he's baggin'.
Oh, just listen to that dragon.
Who's it now he's started slaggin'?

No surprise his tail's not waggin',
Head hung low, whole body saggin'.
Oh, just listen to that dragon
Moanin' so much, he needs gaggin'.

Oh, just listen . . .
Oh, just listen . . .
Oh, just listen to that dragon.

WHAT CAN A DRAGON DO FOR A LIVING?

What can a dragon do for a living?
What can a dragon do?
Not get a job in London Zoo.
Not sell a skirt or a shirt or a shoe.
Not be a porter in Waterloo.
So what can a dragon . . .
What can a dragon . . .
What can a dragon do?

The problem's got him in a proper stew.
He's more hopping mad than a kangaroo.
So what can a dragon . . .
What can a dragon . . .
What can a dragon do?

He could be a cigarette lighter
But he's too big to fit in a pocket.
He could be a plane – say, a fighter –
But he's not got a gun or a rocket.
So what can a dragon . . .
What can a dragon . . .
What can a dragon do?

His breath is a fiery brew.
He could warm your house for you
But the curtains'd certainly scorch
And the furniture blacken like coke.
He might work as a light or torch
Though we'd choke in a cloak of his smoke.
So what can a dragon . . .
What can a dragon . . .
What can a dragon do
To stay off the dole queue?

He could join a security crew.
He could guard the valued possessions
Of those in positions of wealth . . .
But dragons have treasure obsessions
He'd just want it all for himself.
He'd say, 'This stuff is divine. It's ever so fine.
I'm making it mine. You can't have it back!'
So the boss would have to give him the sack.
He'd shout, 'Get out! Get out! Get out!
The dragon's no good! Now, see that he leaves.
How can we have guards who turn into thieves?'
So what can a dragon . . .
What can a dragon . . .
What can a dragon do?

When the summer's well and truly through,
When rain clouds form and a storm is due,
He could be a green umbrella
But he's ever so heavy to hold.
Or maybe a newspaper seller,
But in the freezing cold,
He'd turn from green to blue.
He'd probably get the flu,
And go, 'Achoo! Achoo! Achoo!
This job's no good, I need something new.'
So what can a dragon . . .
What can a dragon . . .
What can a dragon do?
What career can he pursue?

Well, I really wish I knew
But I simply haven't a clue.
What work have we got for the creature?
The problem is proving too tough.
He could have a job as a teacher
But I know he's not nasty enough!
So what can a dragon . . .
What can a dragon . . .
What can a dragon do?
I dunno. Do you?

DUNGEONS AND DRAGONS

When thrown in some deeply dark dungeon
beware of just where you are plunging.
If you smell hungry smoke
It'll be from the throat
Down which you're invited, for luncheon.

If ever you're at such a function
Do try to ignore all that munching.
They make their food suffer
So don't make it tougher
By screaming cos you're who they're crunching.

STORY-TELLING

A dragon from the heart of Wales
Who wears a coat of blood-red scales
With chainsaw teeth and knife-blade nails
Goes raving mad, right off the rails,

Flies northeast to the Yorkshire Dales
On wings as wide as windmill sails
To terrorize those hills and vales,
Slay sheep and feed on their entrails.

So knights are sent, huge-muscled males
Who've rescued maids and hunted Grails.
They've swords and shields and steel chain mails
And armour thick as Thor's thumbnails.

This weighs them down. They move like snails.
So every would-be slayer fails.
The dragon, every time, prevails,
The subject now of dreadful tales.

These focus on the grim details . . .
Each victim's awful dying wails,
Cooked alive when it exhales
Great grilling gusts, volcanic gales.

It's true, I swear! It flew from Wales
Wearing its coat of blood-red scales
With chainsaw teeth and knife-blade nails,
Gone raving mad, right off the rails.

They're tavern-told, these twisted tales.
They're passed around like drinking pails
By ancient Brits and Picts and Gaels,
Their tongues propelled by foaming ales.

While outside, owls and nightingales
And rats and mice with their true tails
Are wise to fiction's flimsy veils.
If lies were crimes, we'd fill our jails.

I'VE SEEN A DRAGON IN FARMER JAMES'S FIELD

Says Dad: There are no dragons now.
You saw Farmer James's cow.

Says I: But, dad, I've never seen
A cow of quite that shade of green.

Says Mum: There are no dragons now.
You saw Farmer James's sow.

Says I: Since when did any pig
Possess a pair of wings that big?

Says Gran: There are no dragons now.
You saw Farmer James's plough.

Says I: If so, then what I saw
Was a plough that had been taught to
roar.

Says Sis: There are no dragons now,
But the farmer's cat has a loud miaow.

Says I: If we've no dragons now,
Then please will someone tell me how
The farmer's cat can breathe out flames
And why it's eating Farmer James.

TRUTH AND LIES
ABOUT DRAGONS

When I look at you,
Can you tell by my eyes
Whether this is true
Or a pack of lies?

Your Chinese dragon, chum, I'll cheerfully confirm
Is a big, bright and blustery, breezy worm.
We had one at school, but it left last term,
Got a good job with a Birmingham firm.

We've bird-like dragons with feathers and beaks
That nest on Peruvian mountain peaks.
They don't hoard treasure, they collect antiques
Acquired from Arabs and shipped by Greeks.

There are sea-serpents in the boiling swell,
Great coiling snakes from the heart of Hell,
That can tell, by smell, where to start an oil well.
They're employed by BP, Gulf and Shell.

Our English dragons inhabit the Shires,
Where everyone admires these graceful flyers.
They start the stubble fires that the squire requires,
And are famed for their fairness as cricket umpires.

Then you've got your Welsh beast, muscly and red,
With skin 'n' bone wings and a brutal head.
Ivor Evans had one in his garden shed,
Though he now grows daffodils and leeks instead.

When I look at you,
Can you tell by my eyes
Whether that was true
Or a pack of lies?

THE CAPTURING OF
A DRAGON

He reared up before me,
His body bright green,
A serpent with legs,
If you know what I mean.

The moment I caught him,
I thought him quite ruthless;
Though dragons have teeth,
And this one was toothless.

His scales were so fine that
They looked just like hair.
His wings were so tiny
They weren't really there.

He wasn't quite able
To demonstrate flight.
His breath wasn't fiery.
It didn't ignite.

And he didn't breathe smoke,
Or let out a roar.
And he hadn't a tail,
Nor a hint of a claw.

He didn't hoard treasure
Or cause maidens grief.
He didn't eat people,
Just chewed on a leaf;

Was not very lengthy,
And not at all tall;
In fact, was not biggish,
But actually quite small.

He lived in a matchbox.
I called him Godzilla . . .
. . . not much of a dragon,
But a great caterpillar!

PARASITES

Far, far away in blue moonlight,
Flocks of dragons are taking flight.
Their scales are dull. Their eyes are bright.
Their teeth are vampire-sharp and white
Like stalactite and stalagmite.

On fields of dreams they'll graze tonight
To satisfy their appetite
For fantasy, far-fetched delight
And magic stories set alight
By wild adventures which excite.

Ours are the dreams on which they'll bite.
From worlds away, and far from sight,
They'll come as guests we don't invite
And read our minds like words we write
And feed on these while we sleep tight.

Our nightmares know this parasite.
With wisps of fear and twists of fright
We've something saying all's not right.
And we'd fight back with all our might
But, locked in sleep, we'll fight no fight.

Far, far away in blue moonlight,
Flocks of dragons are taking flight.
Their scales are dull. Their eyes are bright.
The pain we'll feel will be so slight
From sets of teeth so sharp and white.

THE MAGIC OF DRAGONS

She places aces on her tail,
Impales each with a fingernail,
And every ace becomes a six.
Dragon's doing magic tricks.

She's chucking coins into a pail
But slips each one beneath a scale.
No one spots that it's a fix.
Dragon's doing magic tricks.

Her pyrotechnics never fail.
She breathes on things. They burn, but they'll
Return unburned in just two ticks.
Dragon's doing magic tricks.

She reads our minds like reading Braille.
She's right in every last detail,
Then swallows candles with lit wicks.
Dragon's doing magic tricks.

Pigeons fly from under veils
Through clouds of smoke which she exhales,
Then ropes move up and down two sticks.
Dragon's doing magic tricks.

She introduces Abigail
And saws in half this poor female
But she's restored with two wand-flicks.
Dragon's doing magic tricks.

Wow! I'm amazed. 'It's fake!' you wail.
How sad you are. Go home, telltale,
To walls and floors and life that's stale.
Real homes are more than planks and bricks.
Real lives need dragons, and their tricks.

ALL NIGHT LONG

And all night long our dragon sings
As preciously as diamond rings
Of flaming fragments plucked from strings
And only half-remembered things
And rumours raised on dreamy wings
Like water which the dowser brings
To thirsty lips from long-lost springs.

And all night long our dragon sings
How fate fantastically flings
Time's arrows and outrageous slings
At all our joys and sufferings,
While melody's the sword it swings
At an acrobatic tune that clings
To power . . . just like queens and kings.

And all night long our dragon sings
For us and other underlings
And, through the day, small echoings
Return to strike like tiny stings
Which only cease when evenings
Each darken. Then the dragon sings . . .
And all night long it sings, it sings.

RARE DRAGONS

You'll seldom find a dragon with
No trace of the barbarian,
A sentimental gentle one
Who's not a slightly scary one.

There's surely not a dragon that
Is purely vegetarian,
That really cares for animals
And is a veterinarian.

Or one that looks at lots of books,
A qualified grammarian,
That has a love of literature
And works as a librarian.

No shaven-headed Buddhist nor
Your peaceful, hippy, hairy one,
Nor one that's into reggae who's
A dreadlocked Rastafarian.

HOW WE DEALT WITH DANGEROUS DRAGONS

According
To history's recorders,
Most dragons were hoarders
With wing-spreads as broad as
From here to the borders.
These dangerous marauders
Had mental disorders.

Their victims implored us
And swore to reward us.
They said, 'Please afford us
Help. All have ignored us,
Not even insured us.'

We heard them applaud us
When mad dragons roared as
We caged them, with warders,
The same way the law does:
Big warders with orders
To keep them secured as
Safe as a gun or a sword is.

DRAGONS DON'T EXIST

Dragons, mate? They don't exist.
So cross them off your Christmas list.

We've no such things –
No snakes with wings.

Ask any archaeologist
If dragons do or don't exist.
He'll treat you like you're round the twist.
So pardon me if I insist
That dragons simply don't exist.

We've no such things –
No snakes with wings,
No spikes, no scales,
No pointed tails.

If any college scientist
Suggested that they MIGHT exist
Then he or she would be dismissed.
Not me, cos I'm a realist.
I KNOW that dragons don't exist.

We've no such things –
No snakes with wings,
No spikes, no scales,
No pointed tails,
No sudden death
By fiery breath,

No flying oral arsonist.
'The creature simply can't exist,'
Says teacher and says naturalist.
It's pure Scotch mist so let's desist,
Cos dragons simply don't exist.

We've no such things –
No snakes with wings,
No spikes, no scales,
No pointed tails,
No sudden death
By fiery breath,
No rich rewards,
No treasure hoards.

D R A G O N S

The Blarney Stone must have been kissed
By those insisting they exist.
Oi! See this fist above my wrist?
It's yours right now if you persist,
Cos dragons truly don't exist.

He led us to
The dragon's lair,
Said, 'I'll show you!'
And walked in there.

Then came a roar,
A scream, a moan,
And nothing more
Was ever known

Or missed
Of the man who said dragons
Didn't exist.

CHARLOTTE, EMILY AND ANNE: THE BRONTE-SAURUS SISTERS

Some Yorkshire Dales explorers
Have found these fossils for us:
Three dinosaur señoras,
The sisters Bronte-saurus . . .

. . . which brings us to our chorus
So join in or ignore us
The brontosaurus, brontosaurus, brontosaurus
  chorus.

There's Charlotte Bronte-saurus,
The sort of dinosaur whose
Massively bony jaw has
Teeth like a Labrador has . . .

. . . which brings us to our chorus
So join in or ignore us
The brontosaurus, brontosaurus, brontosaurus
  chorus.

Emily Bronte-saurus,
If still alive would roar as
She pounced on us to claw us
And rip apart and gnaw us . . .

. . . which brings us to our chorus
So join in or ignore us
The brontosaurus, brontosaurus, brontosaurus
    chorus.

Poor Annie Bronte-saurus,
A thousand years before us,
Died of a virus or as
She fought a stegosaurus . . .

. . . which brings us to our chorus
So join in or ignore us
The brontosaurus, brontosaurus, brontosaurus
    chorus.

They died before they saw us
Or heard us do this chorus:
The brontosaurus, brontosaurus, brontosaurus
    chorus.

BONY'S SONG

I'm long. I'm lean.
My skin is green.
My teeth are clean.
My grin is mean.
But mine is not a proper smile.
It's built of bitterness and bile.
And I have got a grim profile
Cos I am not a nice reptile.
I'm Bony, Bony, Bony, Bony,
Bony Crocodile.

It's my delight
To pick a fight.
I'm dynamite.
I claw. I bite.
No, friendliness is not my style.
I play it cool but, all the while,
I'm actually very volatile
Cos I am not a nice reptile.
I'm Bony, Bony, Bony, Bony,
Bony Crocodile.

My jaws are wide,
So slide inside.
We'll take a ride,
A snake-like glide,
A mile or two along the Nile.
I'll leave your bones there in a pile.
Don't pull a face. You know I'm vile
Cos I am not a nice reptile.
I'm Bony, Bony, Bony, Bony,
Bony Crocodile.

BEWARE OF THE GARGOYLE

Your gargoyle, your gargoyle,
You can't trust your gargoyle.
Its tongue and its tail coil.
It watches while you toil.
What it touches will spoil.
Recoil from your gargoyle.

Your gargoyle, your gargoyle,
You can't trust your gargoyle.
Its grin's thin as gold foil.
Where it squats there's turmoil.
No plant grows in that soil.
Recoil from your gargoyle.

Your gargoyle, your gargoyle,
You can't trust your gargoyle.
It's slippery as car oil.
It's dodgy and disloyal.
That beast makes my blood boil.
Recoil from, recoil from,
Recoil from your gargoyle.

NATURE MADE THE ALLIGATOR

Longer, leaner, lighter, straighter,
Nature made the alligator.

Underwater navigator,
Denizen of the Equator,
Bed of reeds or muddy crater.

Longer, leaner, lighter, straighter,
Nature made the alligator.

Made its greed grow ever greater,
Predatory, patient waiter,
Sneaky, silent, prey-locator.

Longer, leaner, lighter, straighter,
Nature made the alligator.

Cool and crafty calculator,
Cruel and creeping infiltrator,
Sudden-action operator.

Longer, leaner, lighter, straighter,
Nature made the alligator.

Animal de-animator,
River-bank depopulator,
Fish-farm thief and devastator.

Longer, leaner, lighter, straighter,
Nature made the alligator.

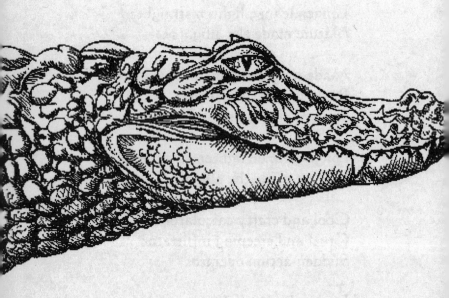

SOME SALAMANDERS

Some salamanders say your name.
Some salamanders pray for fame.
Some salamanders slay and maim.

Some salamanders may show shame.
Some salamanders, they take aim.
Some salamanders sway when lame.

Some salamanders lay the blame.
Some salamanders pay that claim.
Some salamanders weigh the same.

Some salamanders play the game.
Some salamanders stay quite tame.
Some salamanders wade through flame.

DINING OUT WITH DANGER!

When you date an alligator,
Tell the chef and warn the waiter
There and then – it's too late later.
Dwell on it, advise them well.

Say your mate's an alligator,
Spell it out: potato-hater,
Needs raw meat put on the plate or
Eats the staff, and the clientele.

A LOSS OF FLAME AND FLIGHT

When dragon got caught in a blizzard
The weather extinguished his gizzard.
So bitten by frost
That his wings were lost,
He lived on . . . as merely a lizard.

A HAPPY APPETITE

Oh, the crocodile, the crocodile is happy.
And all the while, all the Nile is flappy
Cos a mile of highly sharpened teeth, all gappy,
Are revealed when the crocodile is happy.

Oh, the crocodile, the crocodile is happy.
Yet we know the wily chappy
's friend smile is snappy,
Which is why the silent crocodile is happy.

Oh, the crocodile, the crocodile is happy.
But a silent crocodile is a violent crocodile.
With his vile and toothy trap he
'll slyly satisfy his appy-
-tite. Oh-oh . . . !

The crocodile, the crocodile is happy . . .
'SNAP!'

THE VISITIN' GRIFFIN

We once had a griffin
Turn up to take tiffin
Back at the old place.
A griffin for tiffin!
We all thought: 'How spiffin'!',
Me and the staff and His Grace.

The griffin, a rough 'un,
An uncouth and tough 'un,
Soon proved that that wasn't the case.

I saw His Grace stiffen,
The butler start sniffin',
Then each gave a grim grimace.
One maid went: 'It's niffin'!'
Another: 'It's wiffin'!'
A third simply said: 'That ain't nayce!'

Thus miffin' the griffin
Which, huffin' and puffin',
Raced after them up the staircase.

Now angered, the griffin
Gave butler a biffin'
And, after a bit of chase,
Gave cook quite a duffin',
Claimed: 'I ain't done nuffin'!',
While wiping the blood off cook's chiffon and lace.

'Just listen,' said griffin,
'I'll try to act different,
But gimme a little more space.'

Then, calmly, our griffin
Picked up a fresh muffin
And carried on stuffin' its face.
Disgraced, unforgiven,
That griffin was driven
Away from the place by His Grace.

It's years, now, since we've seen a griffin.
Somewhere, I suppose, they're still livin'.
Thank God, though, they're not commonplace.

THE SURVIVAL OF IVAN THE WYVERN

Meet Ivan the Wyvern.
This dragon's a live 'un,
The last of his kind still surviving.

Ivan, our Wyvern,
Jacks his nine-to-five in,
Convinced his good fortune's reviving.

Ivan the Wyvern
Loves ducking 'n' diving,
And tells us that soon he'll be thriving.
He has this great plan he's contriving:
'The World of Ivan the Wyvern'.

His cave's now a drive-in
That's got an archive in,
A cafe to eat in, a disco to jive in.

But Ivan the Wyvern
Has problems deriving
From half his staff skiving
And rivals conniving
And thereby depriving
His business of funding for fending off bills now
  arriving.

The last bits of loot he's been hiving
Fall short of the thousands he needs to enliven
His fast-fading chance of surviving.
So, pity poor Ivan the Wyvern

WHERE THE SALAMANDER SAT

Oh, a salamander sat in an inferno,
Writing letters to his mother to let her know
That he'd met a lovely lizard in Salerno.
The salamander sat
The salamander sat
The salamander sat in an inferno.

Oh, the salamander sat in an inferno,
He was scribbling away while sipping Pernod
Though I'll never quite know why he didn't burn.
   Oh,
The salamander sat
The salamander sat
The salamander sat in an inferno.

tHE DOG AtE MY BUSPASS

POEMS CHOSEN BY
NICK tOCZEK AND ANDREW FUSEK PEtERS

A brilliant collection of hilarious poems featuring some of the world's most incredible excuses, apologies, tall stories and fibs. It is essential reading for all children (and some adults too!).

from
tHE WORSt EXCUSES iN tHE WORLD

by Clare Bevan

I'd only left it for two minutes while I built a scale model of Buckingham Palace out of cheese triangles, when a whole herd of angry wildebeest stampeded through our back garden, battered down the kitchen door and, before they vanished into the shimmering sunset, trampled my book under their mighty, thundering hoofs, and the dog ate it.

The Monster That Ate the Universe

Poems by Roger Stevens

A glorious collection of poems from the wonderful Roger Stevens, in which he covers subjects as varied as monsters, Halloween, snow, dinosaurs, love, science, parents who dance and chicken school.

CHICKEN SCHOOL

Period one – simple clucking
Period two – more clucking
Period three – clucking with attitude
Period four – clucking with indecision
Period five – pecking in dirt
Period six – pecking in gravel
Period seven – rhythmic and jerky neck movements
Period eight – clucking (revision)

Wizard Poems

**Magical verses, rhymes and spells
chosen by Fiona Waters**

WIZARD POEMS is a marvellous, mighty, mystical and
magical collection packed with advice for young wizards, a
guided tour of Camelot and how to cast a spell to make
your school day shorter.

The Wizard's Book

If you want to read his Spell Book
You must take it by surprise . . .

It watches from the bookshelf
With its fierce and inky eyes
It hears your softest footfall
With its folded paper ears,
It sniffs your fear like perfume,
And it feeds on children's tears.

It lurks in dust and shadows
Where it waits for musty ages
To trap your prying fingers
In its swift and vicious pages,
It tempts you with its secrets
It lures the quick and clever

It lets you think you've won the game
Then snap – you're lost forever!

Clare Bevan

Based on Nick Toczek's best-selling Dragon poems...

Dragons!
The Musical

A dramatic and comical new musical

Words by Nick Toczek • Music by Malcolm Singer

For Key Stages 2 and 3, offering scope to include
younger children and adults.

Fergus is different from all the other kids – he is turning
into a dragon! He and his imaginary friends are taken
through their paces at the School For Dragons, where
they are taught how to speak Dragonese and how to be
as hard as nails! Soon he discovers that he is not the
only person he knows who is also a dragon and that
in fact these fiery fiends are everywhere!

Dragons! contains nine original, exciting and challenging
songs, with optional solos and instrumentals.
A rhyming play is also available, or the songs can
simply be sung as a song cycle for choirs.

The Teacher's Book includes a CD containing
complete performances of all the songs, and imaginative
backing tracks to sing along to.

AVAILABLE SPRING 2005 FROM ALL GOOD PRINTED MUSIC SHOPS!

Teacher's Book and CD: Order No. GA11627
Pupil's Book (containing rhyming play and lyrics): Order No. GA11638

Golden Apple Productions
part of The Music Sales Group
www.musicsales.com